50 Buffalo Sauce Dishes

By: Kelly Johnson

Table of Contents

- Buffalo Chicken Wings
- Buffalo Chicken Dip
- Buffalo Cauliflower Bites
- Buffalo Chicken Wrap
- Buffalo Chicken Salad
- Buffalo Shrimp
- Buffalo Chicken Pizza
- Buffalo Chicken Tenders
- Buffalo Chicken Sliders
- Buffalo Chicken Mac and Cheese
- Buffalo Cauliflower Tacos
- Buffalo Chicken Quesadilla
- Buffalo Chicken Sandwich
- Buffalo Chickpea Wrap
- Buffalo Chicken Stuffed Peppers
- Buffalo Chicken Meatballs
- Buffalo Hummus
- Buffalo Chicken Nachos
- Buffalo Sweet Potato Fries
- Buffalo Chicken Soup
- Buffalo Chicken Baked Potatoes
- Buffalo Roasted Brussels Sprouts
- Buffalo Fried Pickles
- Buffalo Pulled Pork
- Buffalo Chicken Frittata
- Buffalo Chicken Enchiladas
- Buffalo Grilled Cheese
- Buffalo Baked Ziti
- Buffalo Tofu Bites
- Buffalo Chicken Empanadas
- Buffalo Roasted Vegetables
- Buffalo Chicken Chili
- Buffalo Chicken and Rice Casserole
- Buffalo Chicken Skewers
- Buffalo Fries

- Buffalo Chicken Croquettes
- Buffalo Bacon-Wrapped Jalapeños
- Buffalo Shrimp Tacos
- Buffalo Chicken and Blue Cheese Dip
- Buffalo Chicken Lasagna
- Buffalo Chicken Egg Rolls
- Buffalo Bacon-Wrapped Chicken
- Buffalo Chicken Burger
- Buffalo Chicken Tortilla Soup
- Buffalo Potato Skins
- Buffalo Chicken Stir-Fry
- Buffalo Popcorn Chicken
- Buffalo Chicken Casserole
- Buffalo Cauliflower Wings
- Buffalo Grilled Chicken Breast

Buffalo Chicken Wings

Ingredients:

- 10 chicken wings
- 1/4 cup hot sauce (such as Frank's RedHot)
- 2 tablespoons unsalted butter
- 1 tablespoon white vinegar
- 1/2 teaspoon garlic powder
- Salt and pepper to taste
- Blue cheese or ranch dressing for dipping

Instructions:

1. Preheat your oven to 400°F (200°C). Line a baking sheet with parchment paper.
2. Season the chicken wings with salt, pepper, and garlic powder. Place them on the baking sheet.
3. Bake for 25-30 minutes or until the wings are crispy and golden.
4. While the wings bake, combine hot sauce, butter, vinegar, and garlic powder in a small saucepan over medium heat. Stir until the butter melts and the sauce is smooth.
5. Toss the baked wings in the buffalo sauce and serve with blue cheese or ranch dressing on the side.

Buffalo Chicken Dip

Ingredients:

- 2 cups cooked chicken, shredded
- 1 package (8 oz) cream cheese, softened
- 1/2 cup buffalo sauce
- 1/2 cup ranch or blue cheese dressing
- 1 cup shredded cheddar cheese
- 1/2 cup shredded mozzarella cheese
- Celery sticks or tortilla chips for serving

Instructions:

1. Preheat your oven to 350°F (175°C).
2. In a medium mixing bowl, combine the cream cheese, buffalo sauce, ranch or blue cheese dressing, shredded cheddar, and mozzarella cheese.
3. Stir in the shredded chicken and mix until well combined.
4. Transfer the mixture to a baking dish and bake for 20-25 minutes or until the top is golden and bubbly.
5. Serve with celery sticks or tortilla chips for dipping.

Buffalo Cauliflower Bites

Ingredients:

- 1 medium cauliflower, cut into florets
- 1/2 cup flour
- 1/2 cup water
- 1 teaspoon garlic powder
- 1/2 teaspoon paprika
- 1/4 teaspoon salt
- 1/2 cup buffalo sauce
- 1 tablespoon olive oil

Instructions:

1. Preheat your oven to 400°F (200°C). Line a baking sheet with parchment paper.
2. In a mixing bowl, whisk together flour, water, garlic powder, paprika, and salt to create the batter.
3. Dip each cauliflower floret into the batter and place it on the prepared baking sheet.
4. Bake for 20-25 minutes, flipping halfway through, until the cauliflower is crispy.
5. In a separate bowl, toss the baked cauliflower in buffalo sauce and serve with a side of ranch or blue cheese dressing.

Buffalo Chicken Wrap

Ingredients:

- 1 cooked chicken breast, shredded
- 1/4 cup buffalo sauce
- 1 tablespoon ranch or blue cheese dressing
- 1 flour tortilla
- Lettuce
- Sliced tomatoes
- Shredded cheddar cheese

Instructions:

1. In a small bowl, toss the shredded chicken with buffalo sauce and ranch dressing.
2. Lay the tortilla flat on a surface and layer the lettuce, tomatoes, and buffalo chicken mixture in the center.
3. Top with shredded cheddar cheese and roll the tortilla tightly to form a wrap.
4. Serve immediately for a delicious, spicy lunch or snack.

Buffalo Chicken Salad

Ingredients:

- 2 cooked chicken breasts, shredded
- 1/4 cup buffalo sauce
- 1 tablespoon ranch or blue cheese dressing
- Mixed salad greens
- Cherry tomatoes, halved
- Cucumber slices
- Shredded carrots
- Blue cheese crumbles (optional)

Instructions:

1. Toss the shredded chicken with buffalo sauce and ranch dressing in a bowl.
2. Arrange the salad greens, tomatoes, cucumber, and carrots on a large plate or in a bowl.
3. Top the salad with the buffalo chicken and sprinkle with blue cheese crumbles if desired.
4. Serve with extra dressing on the side.

Buffalo Shrimp

Ingredients:

- 1 lb large shrimp, peeled and deveined
- 1/4 cup buffalo sauce
- 2 tablespoons unsalted butter
- 1/2 teaspoon garlic powder
- Salt and pepper to taste
- Fresh parsley for garnish

Instructions:

1. Heat a skillet over medium heat and add butter. Once melted, stir in garlic powder and buffalo sauce.
2. Add the shrimp to the skillet and cook for 3-4 minutes on each side until pink and cooked through.
3. Toss the shrimp in the buffalo sauce and season with salt and pepper.
4. Garnish with fresh parsley and serve hot.

Buffalo Chicken Pizza

Ingredients:

- 1 pizza crust (store-bought or homemade)
- 1/2 cup buffalo sauce
- 1 cup cooked chicken, shredded
- 1/2 cup ranch or blue cheese dressing
- 1 cup shredded mozzarella cheese
- 1/4 cup sliced red onions
- Fresh cilantro for garnish

Instructions:

1. Preheat your oven according to the pizza crust instructions.
2. Spread buffalo sauce over the pizza crust as your base sauce.
3. Top with shredded chicken, mozzarella cheese, and red onions.
4. Bake according to crust instructions, usually for 12-15 minutes until the cheese is melted and bubbly.
5. Drizzle with ranch or blue cheese dressing and garnish with fresh cilantro.

Buffalo Chicken Tenders

Ingredients:

- 4 chicken tenders
- 1/2 cup buffalo sauce
- 1/4 cup flour
- 1/4 teaspoon garlic powder
- 1/4 teaspoon paprika
- Salt and pepper to taste
- Ranch or blue cheese dressing for dipping

Instructions:

1. Preheat your oven to 400°F (200°C). Line a baking sheet with parchment paper.
2. In a bowl, mix the flour, garlic powder, paprika, salt, and pepper. Dredge the chicken tenders in the flour mixture.
3. Place the tenders on the prepared baking sheet and bake for 20-25 minutes, flipping halfway through.
4. While the tenders bake, heat buffalo sauce in a small pan over low heat.
5. Once the chicken tenders are baked, toss them in the buffalo sauce and serve with ranch or blue cheese dressing on the side.

Buffalo Chicken Sliders

Ingredients:

- 2 cups cooked chicken, shredded
- 1/4 cup buffalo sauce
- 2 tablespoons ranch or blue cheese dressing
- 8 slider buns
- 1/2 cup shredded lettuce
- 1/4 cup sliced pickles

Instructions:

1. In a bowl, mix the shredded chicken with buffalo sauce and ranch or blue cheese dressing.
2. Toast the slider buns in a skillet or oven until golden.
3. Spoon the buffalo chicken mixture onto the bottom half of each bun.
4. Top with shredded lettuce and pickles.
5. Place the top half of the buns on the sliders and serve immediately.

Buffalo Chicken Mac and Cheese

Ingredients:

- 2 cups cooked chicken, shredded
- 2 cups elbow macaroni, cooked
- 1/4 cup buffalo sauce
- 2 cups shredded cheddar cheese
- 1/2 cup milk
- 2 tablespoons unsalted butter
- 1 tablespoon flour
- Salt and pepper to taste

Instructions:

1. In a saucepan, melt butter over medium heat. Stir in flour and cook for 1-2 minutes to form a roux.
2. Slowly whisk in milk and bring to a simmer until the sauce thickens.
3. Stir in shredded cheddar cheese and buffalo sauce until smooth.
4. Combine the cooked macaroni, shredded chicken, and buffalo cheese sauce. Stir until well coated.
5. Season with salt and pepper to taste, and serve hot.

Buffalo Cauliflower Tacos

Ingredients:

- 1 medium cauliflower, cut into florets
- 1/2 cup buffalo sauce
- 1 tablespoon olive oil
- 8 small corn tortillas
- Shredded lettuce
- Sliced avocado
- Diced tomatoes
- Cilantro for garnish

Instructions:

1. Preheat the oven to 400°F (200°C). Toss the cauliflower florets with olive oil and buffalo sauce.
2. Spread the cauliflower on a baking sheet and bake for 20-25 minutes, flipping halfway through.
3. Warm the tortillas in a skillet or oven.
4. Assemble the tacos by placing the buffalo cauliflower on the tortillas, then topping with lettuce, avocado, tomatoes, and cilantro.
5. Serve immediately with extra buffalo sauce on the side.

Buffalo Chicken Quesadilla

Ingredients:

- 1 cup cooked chicken, shredded
- 1/4 cup buffalo sauce
- 1/2 cup shredded mozzarella cheese
- 1/4 cup ranch or blue cheese dressing
- 4 flour tortillas
- 1/4 cup chopped green onions
- 1 tablespoon olive oil

Instructions:

1. In a bowl, mix the shredded chicken with buffalo sauce.
2. Heat a skillet over medium heat and add a little olive oil.
3. Place a tortilla in the skillet and top with the buffalo chicken, mozzarella cheese, green onions, and a drizzle of ranch dressing.
4. Place another tortilla on top and cook for 2-3 minutes on each side until golden and the cheese is melted.
5. Slice into wedges and serve with extra ranch or blue cheese dressing.

Buffalo Chicken Sandwich

Ingredients:

- 2 cups cooked chicken, shredded
- 1/4 cup buffalo sauce
- 1 tablespoon mayonnaise
- 2 sandwich buns
- Shredded lettuce
- Sliced tomatoes
- Sliced pickles

Instructions:

1. In a bowl, mix the shredded chicken with buffalo sauce and mayonnaise.
2. Toast the sandwich buns until golden.
3. Layer the buffalo chicken mixture on the bottom half of each bun.
4. Top with shredded lettuce, tomatoes, and pickles.
5. Place the top buns on the sandwiches and serve.

Buffalo Chickpea Wrap

Ingredients:

- 1 can chickpeas, drained and mashed
- 1/4 cup buffalo sauce
- 1 tablespoon tahini or ranch dressing
- 1/4 cup shredded lettuce
- 1/4 cup sliced cucumber
- 1 whole wheat wrap or tortilla

Instructions:

1. In a bowl, mix the mashed chickpeas with buffalo sauce and tahini (or ranch dressing).
2. Lay the wrap flat and layer with shredded lettuce, cucumber, and the buffalo chickpea mixture.
3. Roll up the wrap and serve immediately.

Buffalo Chicken Stuffed Peppers

Ingredients:

- 4 bell peppers, halved and seeded
- 2 cups cooked chicken, shredded
- 1/4 cup buffalo sauce
- 1/2 cup shredded cheddar cheese
- 1 tablespoon olive oil
- Salt and pepper to taste

Instructions:

1. Preheat the oven to 375°F (190°C).
2. Drizzle olive oil over the bell pepper halves and season with salt and pepper. Place them on a baking sheet.
3. In a bowl, mix the shredded chicken with buffalo sauce and stuff the mixture into the pepper halves.
4. Top with shredded cheddar cheese and bake for 20-25 minutes, or until the peppers are tender.
5. Serve hot with extra buffalo sauce on the side.

Buffalo Chicken Meatballs

Ingredients:

- 1 lb ground chicken
- 1/4 cup buffalo sauce
- 1/4 cup breadcrumbs
- 1 egg
- 1 tablespoon parsley, chopped
- 1/2 teaspoon garlic powder
- Salt and pepper to taste

Instructions:

1. Preheat your oven to 400°F (200°C).
2. In a bowl, mix the ground chicken, buffalo sauce, breadcrumbs, egg, parsley, garlic powder, salt, and pepper.
3. Roll the mixture into meatballs and place them on a baking sheet.
4. Bake for 15-20 minutes until golden and cooked through.
5. Serve with ranch or blue cheese dressing.

Buffalo Hummus

Ingredients:

- 1 can chickpeas, drained and rinsed
- 2 tablespoons buffalo sauce
- 1/4 cup tahini
- 2 tablespoons olive oil
- 1 tablespoon lemon juice
- 1/2 teaspoon garlic powder
- Salt and pepper to taste

Instructions:

1. In a food processor, combine chickpeas, buffalo sauce, tahini, olive oil, lemon juice, garlic powder, salt, and pepper.
2. Process until smooth and creamy.
3. Serve with veggies, pita chips, or crackers for dipping.

Buffalo Chicken Nachos

Ingredients:

- 2 cups cooked chicken, shredded
- 1/4 cup buffalo sauce
- 1 bag tortilla chips
- 1 cup shredded cheddar cheese
- 1/2 cup shredded mozzarella cheese
- 1/4 cup sliced green onions
- 1/4 cup crumbled blue cheese
- 1/4 cup sour cream
- 1 tablespoon chopped cilantro (optional)

Instructions:

1. Preheat the oven to 375°F (190°C).
2. In a bowl, toss the shredded chicken with buffalo sauce until well coated.
3. Spread the tortilla chips on a baking sheet and layer with the buffalo chicken, cheddar cheese, and mozzarella cheese.
4. Bake in the oven for 10-15 minutes, or until the cheese is melted and bubbly.
5. Remove from the oven and top with green onions, crumbled blue cheese, sour cream, and cilantro.
6. Serve immediately.

Buffalo Sweet Potato Fries

Ingredients:

- 2 large sweet potatoes, cut into fries
- 2 tablespoons olive oil
- 1/4 cup buffalo sauce
- Salt and pepper to taste
- 1/4 cup ranch dressing or blue cheese dressing (for dipping)

Instructions:

1. Preheat the oven to 400°F (200°C).
2. Toss the sweet potato fries with olive oil, salt, and pepper, then spread them evenly on a baking sheet.
3. Bake for 25-30 minutes, flipping halfway through, until crispy and golden.
4. Drizzle the buffalo sauce over the fries and toss to coat.
5. Serve with ranch or blue cheese dressing for dipping.

Buffalo Chicken Soup

Ingredients:

- 2 cups cooked chicken, shredded
- 1 tablespoon olive oil
- 1 small onion, chopped
- 2 cloves garlic, minced
- 1/4 cup buffalo sauce
- 4 cups chicken broth
- 1 cup heavy cream
- 1 cup shredded cheddar cheese
- Salt and pepper to taste
- Chopped green onions for garnish

Instructions:

1. In a large pot, heat olive oil over medium heat. Add chopped onion and garlic, and sauté for 3-4 minutes until softened.
2. Add the shredded chicken and buffalo sauce, stirring to combine.
3. Pour in the chicken broth and bring to a simmer. Cook for 10 minutes.
4. Stir in the heavy cream and shredded cheddar cheese, and cook until the cheese is melted and the soup is creamy.
5. Season with salt and pepper to taste, and garnish with chopped green onions.
6. Serve hot.

Buffalo Chicken Baked Potatoes

Ingredients:

- 4 large russet potatoes, baked
- 2 cups cooked chicken, shredded
- 1/4 cup buffalo sauce
- 1/4 cup sour cream
- 1/4 cup shredded cheddar cheese
- 1/4 cup chopped green onions
- 1/4 cup crumbled blue cheese (optional)

Instructions:

1. Bake the russet potatoes at 400°F (200°C) for 45-50 minutes, or until tender.
2. In a bowl, toss the shredded chicken with buffalo sauce.
3. Cut the baked potatoes in half and fluff the insides with a fork.
4. Spoon the buffalo chicken onto the potatoes.
5. Top with sour cream, shredded cheddar cheese, green onions, and crumbled blue cheese.
6. Serve immediately.

Buffalo Roasted Brussels Sprouts

Ingredients:

- 1 lb Brussels sprouts, trimmed and halved
- 2 tablespoons olive oil
- 1/4 cup buffalo sauce
- Salt and pepper to taste
- Chopped green onions for garnish

Instructions:

1. Preheat the oven to 400°F (200°C).
2. Toss the Brussels sprouts with olive oil, salt, and pepper, and spread them on a baking sheet.
3. Roast in the oven for 20-25 minutes, or until crispy and golden, flipping halfway through.
4. Drizzle with buffalo sauce and toss to coat.
5. Garnish with chopped green onions and serve.

Buffalo Fried Pickles

Ingredients:

- 1 jar pickle spears or chips
- 1/2 cup flour
- 1/2 cup cornmeal
- 1/4 teaspoon garlic powder
- 1/4 teaspoon paprika
- Salt and pepper to taste
- 1/4 cup buffalo sauce
- 1 egg, beaten
- Oil for frying
- Ranch or blue cheese dressing for dipping

Instructions:

1. Heat oil in a deep pan over medium-high heat.
2. In a bowl, mix the flour, cornmeal, garlic powder, paprika, salt, and pepper.
3. Dip the pickle spears or chips into the beaten egg, then dredge them in the flour mixture.
4. Fry the pickles in the hot oil for 2-3 minutes, or until golden and crispy.
5. Remove the pickles from the oil and toss them with buffalo sauce.
6. Serve with ranch or blue cheese dressing for dipping.

Buffalo Pulled Pork

Ingredients:

- 2 lbs pork shoulder
- 1/2 cup buffalo sauce
- 1/4 cup apple cider vinegar
- 1 tablespoon brown sugar
- 1 tablespoon garlic powder
- 1 teaspoon onion powder
- Salt and pepper to taste
- Slider buns or sandwich rolls

Instructions:

1. Preheat the slow cooker to low. Season the pork shoulder with salt, pepper, garlic powder, and onion powder.
2. Place the pork shoulder in the slow cooker and add buffalo sauce, apple cider vinegar, and brown sugar.
3. Cover and cook on low for 6-8 hours, or until the pork is tender and can be shredded with a fork.
4. Shred the pork using two forks and toss it in the sauce.
5. Serve on slider buns or sandwich rolls with additional buffalo sauce.

Buffalo Chicken Frittata

Ingredients:

- 2 cups cooked chicken, shredded
- 1/4 cup buffalo sauce
- 8 large eggs
- 1/4 cup milk
- 1/2 cup shredded cheddar cheese
- 1/4 cup chopped green onions
- Salt and pepper to taste

Instructions:

1. Preheat the oven to 375°F (190°C).
2. In a bowl, whisk together eggs, milk, salt, and pepper.
3. In a skillet, combine the shredded chicken and buffalo sauce, then cook over medium heat for 2-3 minutes.
4. Pour the egg mixture over the chicken and stir to combine.
5. Sprinkle with cheddar cheese and green onions, then transfer the skillet to the oven.
6. Bake for 20-25 minutes, or until the frittata is set and golden.
7. Serve hot.

Buffalo Chicken Enchiladas

Ingredients:

- 2 cups cooked chicken, shredded
- 1/4 cup buffalo sauce
- 8 flour tortillas
- 1 cup shredded cheddar cheese
- 1 cup shredded mozzarella cheese
- 1/2 cup ranch dressing
- 1/4 cup chopped green onions
- Salt and pepper to taste

Instructions:

1. Preheat the oven to 375°F (190°C).
2. In a bowl, combine the shredded chicken with buffalo sauce. Season with salt and pepper.
3. Warm the tortillas slightly to make them more pliable, then fill each with buffalo chicken and a sprinkle of cheese.
4. Roll up the tortillas and place them seam-side down in a baking dish.
5. Top with the remaining cheddar and mozzarella cheeses, then bake for 20-25 minutes, or until the cheese is melted and bubbly.
6. Drizzle with ranch dressing and sprinkle with green onions before serving.

Buffalo Grilled Cheese

Ingredients:

- 2 slices of bread
- 1 tablespoon butter
- 1/4 cup buffalo sauce
- 1/2 cup shredded cheddar cheese
- 1/2 cup mozzarella cheese
- 1/2 cup cooked chicken, shredded

Instructions:

1. Preheat a skillet over medium heat.
2. Butter one side of each slice of bread. Place one slice, butter-side down, in the skillet.
3. Top with buffalo sauce, shredded chicken, cheddar, and mozzarella.
4. Place the second slice of bread on top, butter-side up.
5. Grill for 3-4 minutes per side, or until the bread is golden brown and the cheese is melted.
6. Serve immediately.

Buffalo Baked Ziti

Ingredients:

- 1 lb ziti pasta
- 2 cups cooked chicken, shredded
- 1/4 cup buffalo sauce
- 1 cup marinara sauce
- 2 cups ricotta cheese
- 2 cups shredded mozzarella cheese
- 1/4 cup grated Parmesan cheese
- Salt and pepper to taste

Instructions:

1. Preheat the oven to 375°F (190°C).
2. Cook the ziti pasta according to package directions. Drain and set aside.
3. In a bowl, mix the shredded chicken with buffalo sauce and marinara sauce.
4. In a separate bowl, combine the ricotta cheese with salt and pepper.
5. In a large baking dish, layer pasta, buffalo chicken mixture, ricotta cheese, and shredded mozzarella. Repeat the layers.
6. Top with grated Parmesan and bake for 25-30 minutes, until bubbly and golden.
7. Serve hot.

Buffalo Tofu Bites

Ingredients:

- 1 block firm tofu, drained and cubed
- 1/4 cup buffalo sauce
- 1/4 cup flour
- 1 tablespoon cornstarch
- 1/2 teaspoon garlic powder
- Salt and pepper to taste
- Oil for frying

Instructions:

1. In a bowl, toss the tofu cubes with buffalo sauce and let them marinate for 10-15 minutes.
2. In a separate bowl, mix flour, cornstarch, garlic powder, salt, and pepper.
3. Heat oil in a skillet over medium-high heat.
4. Dredge the tofu cubes in the flour mixture, then fry in the hot oil for 3-4 minutes on each side, or until golden and crispy.
5. Drain on paper towels and serve with dipping sauce.

Buffalo Chicken Empanadas

Ingredients:

- 2 cups cooked chicken, shredded
- 1/4 cup buffalo sauce
- 1 package empanada dough discs
- 1 cup shredded cheddar cheese
- 1 egg, beaten
- Salt and pepper to taste

Instructions:

1. Preheat the oven to 375°F (190°C).
2. Mix the shredded chicken with buffalo sauce and season with salt and pepper.
3. Place a spoonful of the buffalo chicken mixture in the center of each empanada disc.
4. Sprinkle with cheddar cheese and fold the dough over to create a half-moon shape.
5. Seal the edges by pressing with a fork, then brush the tops with beaten egg.
6. Bake for 20-25 minutes, until golden brown.
7. Serve hot.

Buffalo Roasted Vegetables

Ingredients:

- 1 lb mixed vegetables (carrots, cauliflower, broccoli, etc.)
- 1/4 cup buffalo sauce
- 2 tablespoons olive oil
- Salt and pepper to taste
- Chopped green onions for garnish

Instructions:

1. Preheat the oven to 400°F (200°C).
2. Toss the vegetables with olive oil, salt, pepper, and buffalo sauce.
3. Spread the vegetables evenly on a baking sheet.
4. Roast for 20-25 minutes, or until tender and slightly crispy.
5. Garnish with chopped green onions and serve immediately.

Buffalo Chicken Chili

Ingredients:

- 2 cups cooked chicken, shredded
- 1/4 cup buffalo sauce
- 1 onion, chopped
- 1 bell pepper, chopped
- 1 can (15 oz) diced tomatoes
- 1 can (15 oz) kidney beans, drained and rinsed
- 2 cups chicken broth
- 1 teaspoon chili powder
- 1/2 teaspoon cumin
- Salt and pepper to taste

Instructions:

1. In a large pot, sauté the onion and bell pepper until softened.
2. Add the shredded chicken, buffalo sauce, diced tomatoes, kidney beans, chicken broth, chili powder, and cumin.
3. Bring to a simmer and cook for 20-30 minutes, stirring occasionally.
4. Season with salt and pepper to taste.
5. Serve hot, garnished with cheese or green onions if desired.

Buffalo Chicken and Rice Casserole

Ingredients:

- 2 cups cooked chicken, shredded
- 1 cup rice, cooked
- 1/4 cup buffalo sauce
- 1 cup shredded cheddar cheese
- 1/2 cup sour cream
- 1/2 cup chopped green onions
- Salt and pepper to taste

Instructions:

1. Preheat the oven to 375°F (190°C).
2. In a large bowl, mix together the shredded chicken, cooked rice, buffalo sauce, sour cream, and 1/2 of the shredded cheddar cheese.
3. Season with salt and pepper.
4. Transfer the mixture to a greased baking dish and top with the remaining cheddar cheese.
5. Bake for 20-25 minutes, or until the cheese is melted and bubbly.
6. Garnish with chopped green onions before serving.

Buffalo Chicken Skewers

Ingredients:

- 2 cups cooked chicken, cubed
- 1/4 cup buffalo sauce
- 1 tablespoon olive oil
- 1/2 teaspoon garlic powder
- Salt and pepper to taste
- Wooden skewers (soaked in water for 10 minutes)

Instructions:

1. Preheat the grill to medium-high heat.
2. In a bowl, toss the chicken cubes with buffalo sauce, olive oil, garlic powder, salt, and pepper.
3. Thread the chicken onto the soaked skewers.
4. Grill the skewers for 4-5 minutes on each side, or until the chicken is heated through and slightly charred.
5. Serve hot with a side of ranch or blue cheese dressing for dipping.

Buffalo Fries

Ingredients:

- 4 large potatoes, cut into fries
- 1/4 cup buffalo sauce
- 2 tablespoons olive oil
- Salt to taste
- 1/2 cup blue cheese dressing
- Chopped green onions for garnish

Instructions:

1. Preheat the oven to 425°F (220°C). Line a baking sheet with parchment paper.
2. Toss the potato fries in olive oil and season with salt.
3. Spread the fries in a single layer on the baking sheet and bake for 25-30 minutes, or until crispy and golden brown.
4. Drizzle buffalo sauce over the fries and toss to coat evenly.
5. Serve with blue cheese dressing and garnish with chopped green onions.

Buffalo Chicken Croquettes

Ingredients:

- 2 cups cooked chicken, shredded
- 1/4 cup buffalo sauce
- 1/2 cup breadcrumbs
- 1 egg, beaten
- 1/2 cup flour
- Salt and pepper to taste
- Oil for frying

Instructions:

1. In a bowl, combine the shredded chicken, buffalo sauce, breadcrumbs, salt, and pepper. Mix well.
2. Shape the mixture into small croquettes or balls.
3. Dredge each croquette in flour, dip in the beaten egg, then coat in breadcrumbs.
4. Heat oil in a frying pan over medium heat.
5. Fry the croquettes for 3-4 minutes on each side, until golden and crispy.
6. Serve hot with ranch or blue cheese dipping sauce.

Buffalo Bacon-Wrapped Jalapeños

Ingredients:

- 12 jalapeños, halved and seeded
- 6 slices bacon, cut in half
- 1/4 cup buffalo sauce
- 1/2 cup cream cheese
- 1/4 cup shredded cheddar cheese
- Salt and pepper to taste

Instructions:

1. Preheat the oven to 375°F (190°C).
2. Mix the cream cheese, buffalo sauce, shredded cheddar, salt, and pepper in a bowl.
3. Stuff each jalapeño half with the buffalo cream cheese mixture.
4. Wrap each stuffed jalapeño with a half slice of bacon and secure with toothpicks.
5. Place the jalapeños on a baking sheet and bake for 20-25 minutes, until the bacon is crispy and the filling is bubbly.
6. Serve immediately.

Buffalo Shrimp Tacos

Ingredients:

- 1 lb shrimp, peeled and deveined
- 1/4 cup buffalo sauce
- 1 tablespoon olive oil
- 8 small corn tortillas
- 1/2 cup shredded lettuce
- 1/4 cup blue cheese crumbles
- 1/4 cup diced tomatoes
- Lime wedges for serving

Instructions:

1. In a bowl, toss the shrimp with buffalo sauce and olive oil.
2. Heat a skillet over medium heat and cook the shrimp for 2-3 minutes per side, until pink and cooked through.
3. Warm the corn tortillas in a pan or microwave.
4. To assemble the tacos, place a few shrimp on each tortilla, then top with shredded lettuce, blue cheese, and diced tomatoes.
5. Serve with lime wedges for squeezing.

Buffalo Chicken and Blue Cheese Dip

Ingredients:

- 2 cups cooked chicken, shredded
- 1/4 cup buffalo sauce
- 8 oz cream cheese, softened
- 1/2 cup sour cream
- 1/2 cup blue cheese crumbles
- 1/2 cup shredded cheddar cheese
- Chopped green onions for garnish
- Tortilla chips or celery for dipping

Instructions:

1. Preheat the oven to 350°F (175°C).
2. In a bowl, combine the shredded chicken with buffalo sauce, cream cheese, sour cream, blue cheese, and shredded cheddar.
3. Spread the mixture into a baking dish and bake for 20-25 minutes, until bubbly and golden.
4. Garnish with chopped green onions and serve with tortilla chips or celery for dipping.

Buffalo Chicken Lasagna

Ingredients:

- 2 cups cooked chicken, shredded
- 1/4 cup buffalo sauce
- 12 lasagna noodles, cooked
- 1/2 cup ricotta cheese
- 2 cups shredded mozzarella cheese
- 1/2 cup shredded cheddar cheese
- 1 cup marinara sauce
- 1 tablespoon olive oil
- 1/4 cup chopped green onions

Instructions:

1. Preheat the oven to 375°F (190°C).
2. In a bowl, mix the shredded chicken with buffalo sauce.
3. In a baking dish, spread a thin layer of marinara sauce on the bottom. Layer with cooked lasagna noodles, followed by a layer of buffalo chicken, ricotta cheese, shredded mozzarella, and cheddar cheese.
4. Repeat the layers and finish with mozzarella and cheddar cheese on top.
5. Cover with foil and bake for 30 minutes, then remove the foil and bake for another 10 minutes until bubbly and golden.
6. Garnish with chopped green onions and serve.

Buffalo Chicken Egg Rolls

Ingredients:

- 2 cups cooked chicken, shredded
- 1/4 cup buffalo sauce
- 1/2 cup shredded mozzarella cheese
- 1/4 cup blue cheese crumbles
- 12 egg roll wrappers
- Oil for frying

Instructions:

1. In a bowl, combine the shredded chicken with buffalo sauce, mozzarella cheese, and blue cheese crumbles.
2. Lay an egg roll wrapper on a flat surface, place a spoonful of the buffalo chicken mixture in the center, and fold the edges to seal.
3. Heat oil in a frying pan over medium heat.
4. Fry the egg rolls for 3-4 minutes per side, until golden and crispy.
5. Drain on paper towels and serve hot with ranch or blue cheese dipping sauce.

Buffalo Bacon-Wrapped Chicken

Ingredients:

- 4 boneless, skinless chicken breasts
- 1/4 cup buffalo sauce
- 8 slices bacon
- 1/4 cup blue cheese crumbles
- 1 tablespoon olive oil
- Salt and pepper to taste

Instructions:

1. Preheat the oven to 375°F (190°C).
2. Season the chicken breasts with salt and pepper, then drizzle with buffalo sauce.
3. Wrap each chicken breast with 2 slices of bacon, securing with toothpicks if needed.
4. Heat olive oil in an ovenproof skillet over medium-high heat.
5. Sear the bacon-wrapped chicken for 3-4 minutes on each side, then transfer the skillet to the oven.
6. Bake for 20-25 minutes, until the chicken is cooked through and the bacon is crispy.
7. Sprinkle with blue cheese crumbles and serve.

Buffalo Chicken Burger

Ingredients:

- 1 lb ground chicken
- 1/4 cup buffalo sauce
- 1/4 cup breadcrumbs
- 1/4 cup finely chopped onions
- 1/4 cup shredded cheddar cheese
- Salt and pepper to taste
- 4 hamburger buns
- Lettuce, tomato, and blue cheese dressing for toppings

Instructions:

1. In a bowl, mix the ground chicken with buffalo sauce, breadcrumbs, onions, cheddar cheese, salt, and pepper.
2. Form the mixture into 4 patties.
3. Heat a grill or skillet over medium heat and cook the patties for 5-6 minutes on each side until fully cooked.
4. Toast the hamburger buns and assemble the burgers with lettuce, tomato, and blue cheese dressing.
5. Serve immediately and enjoy!

Buffalo Chicken Tortilla Soup

Ingredients:

- 2 cups cooked chicken, shredded
- 4 cups chicken broth
- 1/4 cup buffalo sauce
- 1 can diced tomatoes
- 1 can corn kernels, drained
- 1 cup black beans, drained and rinsed
- 1 small onion, diced
- 2 cloves garlic, minced
- 1 teaspoon cumin
- 1/2 teaspoon chili powder
- Salt and pepper to taste
- Tortilla chips, shredded cheese, and sour cream for garnish

Instructions:

1. In a large pot, sauté the onions and garlic in a bit of olive oil until softened.
2. Add the shredded chicken, chicken broth, buffalo sauce, diced tomatoes, corn, black beans, cumin, and chili powder.
3. Bring the soup to a simmer and cook for 15-20 minutes, letting the flavors meld together.
4. Season with salt and pepper to taste.
5. Serve the soup in bowls, garnished with tortilla chips, shredded cheese, and sour cream.

Buffalo Potato Skins

Ingredients:

- 4 large russet potatoes, baked and halved
- 1/2 cup cooked chicken, shredded
- 1/4 cup buffalo sauce
- 1/2 cup shredded cheddar cheese
- 1/4 cup blue cheese crumbles
- 2 tablespoons sour cream
- Chopped green onions for garnish

Instructions:

1. Preheat the oven to 375°F (190°C).
2. Scoop out the insides of the baked potato halves, leaving a thin border around the edge.
3. Mix the shredded chicken with buffalo sauce and stuff the potato skins with the mixture.
4. Top each potato skin with shredded cheddar cheese and bake for 15 minutes, until the cheese is melted.
5. Garnish with blue cheese crumbles, sour cream, and chopped green onions.

Buffalo Chicken Stir-Fry

Ingredients:

- 1 lb chicken breast, cut into thin strips
- 1/4 cup buffalo sauce
- 1 tablespoon soy sauce
- 1 tablespoon olive oil
- 1 red bell pepper, sliced
- 1 yellow bell pepper, sliced
- 1 small onion, sliced

- 2 cloves garlic, minced
- Salt and pepper to taste
- Cooked rice for serving

Instructions:

1. Heat the olive oil in a large skillet over medium-high heat.
2. Add the chicken strips and cook until browned and cooked through, about 5-6 minutes.
3. Add the garlic and sliced bell peppers to the skillet, cooking for another 2-3 minutes until softened.
4. Stir in the buffalo sauce and soy sauce, and cook for another minute.
5. Season with salt and pepper to taste and serve over cooked rice.

Buffalo Popcorn Chicken

Ingredients:

- 1 lb chicken breast, cut into bite-sized pieces
- 1/2 cup buffalo sauce
- 1 cup breadcrumbs
- 1/2 cup flour
- 2 eggs, beaten
- 1/2 teaspoon paprika
- Salt and pepper to taste
- Oil for frying

Instructions:

1. In a bowl, season the chicken pieces with salt, pepper, and paprika.
2. Dredge the chicken in flour, dip in beaten eggs, and coat with breadcrumbs.
3. Heat oil in a frying pan over medium-high heat.
4. Fry the chicken pieces in batches until golden brown and crispy, about 3-4 minutes per side.
5. Toss the fried chicken in buffalo sauce and serve with ranch or blue cheese dipping sauce.

Buffalo Chicken Casserole

Ingredients:

- 2 cups cooked chicken, shredded
- 1 cup buffalo sauce
- 1 cup cooked pasta (penne or rotini works best)
- 1/2 cup sour cream
- 1 cup shredded mozzarella cheese
- 1/2 cup shredded cheddar cheese
- 1/4 cup chopped green onions for garnish

Instructions:

1. Preheat the oven to 350°F (175°C).
2. In a large bowl, combine the shredded chicken, buffalo sauce, sour cream, cooked pasta, and shredded mozzarella cheese.
3. Transfer the mixture to a greased baking dish and top with shredded cheddar cheese.
4. Bake for 20-25 minutes, until the casserole is bubbly and the cheese is melted.
5. Garnish with chopped green onions and serve.

Buffalo Cauliflower Wings

Ingredients:

- 1 large cauliflower, cut into florets
- 1/4 cup buffalo sauce
- 1/4 cup olive oil
- 1 tablespoon cornstarch
- Salt and pepper to taste
- Ranch or blue cheese dressing for dipping

Instructions:

1. Preheat the oven to 425°F (220°C) and line a baking sheet with parchment paper.
2. In a bowl, mix the buffalo sauce, olive oil, cornstarch, salt, and pepper.
3. Toss the cauliflower florets in the sauce mixture until evenly coated.
4. Arrange the cauliflower on the baking sheet and bake for 20-25 minutes, turning halfway, until crispy.

5. Serve with ranch or blue cheese dressing.

Buffalo Grilled Chicken Breast

Ingredients:

- 4 boneless, skinless chicken breasts
- 1/4 cup buffalo sauce
- 2 tablespoons olive oil
- 1 tablespoon garlic powder
- 1 tablespoon onion powder
- Salt and pepper to taste

Instructions:

1. Preheat the grill to medium-high heat.
2. Brush the chicken breasts with olive oil and season with garlic powder, onion powder, salt, and pepper.
3. Grill the chicken for 6-7 minutes per side until fully cooked and the internal temperature reaches 165°F (75°C).
4. During the last minute of grilling, brush the chicken with buffalo sauce.
5. Serve with your favorite sides.

www.ingramcontent.com/pod-product-compliance
Lightning Source LLC
LaVergne TN
LVHW081508060526
838201LV00056BA/3010